Editor
Eric Migliaccio

Managing Editor
Ina Massler Levin, M.A.

Editor-in-Chief
Sharon Coan, M.S. Ed.

Cover Artist
Barb Lorseyedi

Art Manager
Kevin Barnes

Imaging
James Edward Grace

Product Manager
Phil Garcia

Publisher
Mary D. Smith, M.S. Ed.

Main Idea

GRADE 4

Includes practice for Standardized Tests

Author

Debra J. Housel, M.S. Ed.

Teacher Created Resources, Inc.
6421 Industry Way
Westminster, CA 92683
www.teachercreated.com

ISBN: 978-0-7439-8644-1

©*2004 Teacher Created Resources, Inc.*
Reprinted, 2009
Made in U.S.A.

Table of Contents

Introduction

The old adage "practice makes perfect" can apply to your child and his or her education. The more practice and exposure your child has with concepts being taught in school, the more success he or she is likely to find. For many parents, knowing how to help their children may be frustrating because the resources may not be readily available. As a parent, it is also hard to know where to focus your efforts so that the extra practice your child receives at home supports what he or she is learning in school.

A child's ability to understand what he or she reads depends largely upon the ability to locate the main idea of a passage and identify the details that support it. *Practice Makes Perfect: Main Idea* covers identifying the main idea and supporting details in both fiction and nonfiction text. To allow for the greatest variety of practice, the passages are not complete stories. The exercises included in this book meet or reinforce educational standards and objectives similar to the ones required by your state and school district for fourth graders:

☞ The student will identify the main idea in fiction and nonfiction text.

☞ The student will locate supporting details in fiction and nonfiction text.

☞ The student will identify the topic sentence in a passage.

☞ The student will choose the best title for a passage.

☞ The student will summarize the main idea of a passage.

Introduction *(cont.)*

How to Make the Most of This Book

☞ Set aside a specific place in your home to work on this book. Keep the necessary materials on hand.

☞ Determine a specific time of day to work on these practice pages to establish consistency. Look for times in your day or week that are conducive to practicing skills.

☞ Keep all practice sessions with your child positive and constructive. If your child becomes frustrated or tense, set aside the book and look for another time to practice. Do not force your child to perform or use this book as a punishment.

☞ Allow the child to use whatever writing instrument he or she prefers.

☞ Review and praise the work your child has done.

Things to Remember About the Main Idea in Nonfiction

Make certain that your child understands the way that authors typically present ideas in nonfiction materials. Nonfiction writers use four different paragraph structures. In order of frequency, these paragraph structures are:

Paragraph Structure #1

Usually the main idea is directly stated as the first sentence of a paragraph. The rest of the paragraph provides the supporting details:

> *Clara Barton, known as America's first nurse, was a brave and devoted humanitarian.* While caring for others, she was shot at, got frostbitten fingers, had severe laryngitis twice, burned her hands, and almost lost her eyesight. Yet she continued to care for the sick and injured until she died at the age of 91.

Paragraph Structure #2

Once in a while the main idea may be in the center of the paragraph, surrounded on both sides by details:

> The coral have created a reef where more than 200 kinds of birds and about 1,500 types of fish live. *In fact, Australia's Great Barrier Reef provides a home for a great variety of interesting animals.* These include sea turtles, giant clams, crabs, and crown-of-thorns starfish.

Paragraph Structure #3

Often the main idea comes at the end of the paragraph as a summary of the details that came before:

> Each year Antarctica spends six months in darkness, from mid-March to mid-September. The continent is covered year-round by ice, which causes sunlight to reflect off its surface. It never really warms up. The coldest temperature ever recorded on Earth was in Antarctica. *Antarctica has one of the harshest environments in the world.*

Introduction *(cont.)*

Things to Remember About the Main Idea in Non-Fiction *(cont.)*

Paragraph Structure #4

Sometimes the main idea is not directly stated and must be inferred from the details given in the paragraph. This paragraph structure is the most challenging and the least common in nonfiction text for children:

> The biggest sea horse ever found was over a foot long. Large sea horses live along the coasts of New Zealand, Australia, and California. Smaller sea horses live off the coast of Florida, in the Caribbean Sea, and in the Gulf of Mexico. The smallest adult sea horse ever found was only one-half-inch long!

In this example, the implied main idea is that sea horses' sizes vary based on where they live.

When the main idea isn't stated, the student must pull together the details to ascertain the key idea. A good way to do this is to think about the "reporter questions": who, (did) what, when, where, why, and how. The passage may present the answers in any order; however, not all of the questions are always answered.

Things to Remember About the Main Idea in Fiction

☞ Unlike nonfiction text, literature rarely has paragraphs with topic sentences and supporting details. Often in fictional text the main idea is never directly stated anywhere in the passage. This can present a challenging task for your young student. One of the best ways for a student to ascertain the main idea in fiction is to form a movie in his or her mind. This changing visualization will help the child to figure out the key idea.

☞ Just as they do in nonfiction, the answers to the questions *who, did what, when, where, why,* and *how* lead a reader to the details in fiction. A compilation of the details can also be helpful in identifying the main idea. Even so, without a topic sentence, stating the main idea requires paraphrasing, which is a higher-level thinking skill.

☞ In literature, the main idea is often embedded in emotions the emotions of the characters and the emotions of the reader. Well-written fiction makes the reader feel as if he or she is there and actually experiencing the events in the story. Therefore, encourage your student to notice the emotions of the characters. Ask leading questions such as, How would you feel if you were [character s name]? Why? Do you think [character s name] feels like you do? Why?

The main idea is what a paragraph or passage is about overall. It is frequently stated in a sentence and then supported by details within the paragraph.

Passage 1

You know that predators need prey. But did you know that prey also needs predators? It seems unbelievable until you consider this true story. In the 1920s a pair of moose swam out to an island in Lake Superior. Since they were the only big animals there, by 1930 their population had grown to 3,000! That many moose ate the plants faster than the plants could grow back. In 1933 the moose began to starve to death. With fewer moose, the plants grew back. Over time the moose population started growing again. Since there were still no predators for the moose, there got to be too many. They began to starve again.

Then a pair of wolves swam out to the island. They ate the moose. Now there were fewer moose. However, the number of wolves grew. When there got to be too many wolves, they started to starve. After many years a balance of 600 moose and 20 wolves lived on the island. There were just enough moose and just enough wolves to keep them both from starving.

What is the main idea?

ⓐ Prey needs predators just as much as predators need prey.

ⓑ Moose and wolves live on an island in Lake Superior.

ⓒ Too few wolves for the number of moose result in the moose starving.

ⓓ Too many wolves for the number of moose result in the wolves starving.

Passage 2

Although they tried to move quietly, with each step it seemed that a twig snapped or leaves crunched under the men's feet. "This is hopeless," Jon thought. "Every creature within a mile must hear us coming. We'll never catch a turkey for our table if we make all this racket."

What is the main idea?

ⓐ Jon and other men are creeping up on some turkeys.

ⓑ The turkeys are listening to the people as they walk.

ⓒ Jon worries that they won't get to eat turkey.

ⓓ Jon and the others are trying to make a lot of noise.

Passage 3

During the winter the only polar bears that stay in dens are pregnant or nursing mothers.

Since there's a steady supply of food, the rest of the polar bears stay active in winter. They eat seals and walruses. Polar bears must eat a lot because they have big bodies. They are the biggest of all bears. In fact, a full-grown polar bear can weigh over half a ton and stand 10 feet tall on its hind legs.

When the ice melts in the spring, most polar bears dig down in the soil to a layer of permanently frozen soil. They rest in these dens until they can easily locate food. This lets them survive when food is scarce for months at a time.

What is the main idea?

ⓐ Polar bears have different winter and summer dens.

ⓑ Polar bears eat a lot during winter but little or nothing during the rest of the year.

ⓒ Pregnant and nursing polar bears stay inside dens during the winter.

ⓓ Polar bears must eat a lot to maintain their large size.

Passage 4

The angry wild boar attacked the lion, jabbing at him with his sharp, pointed tusks. The lion lunged at the wild boar's throat, dug in with his teeth, and wouldn't let go. The hot sun beat down on the pair until they could bear no more. They both backed away from each other, tired and thirsty, one to each side of the pool. Each was injured, although not fatally. It was evident that once they regained their strength their fight would continue.

As he rested, licking his wounds, the lion looked up at a nearby tree. There, watching and waiting, sat a flock of large vultures. They were eager to feast on whoever lost the battle.

What is the main idea?

ⓐ The angry wild boar attacked the lion first.

ⓑ The lion dug its teeth into the boar's throat.

ⓒ The two injured animals take a break from their fight.

ⓓ A lion and wild boar battle while vultures wait to eat the loser.

Passage 5

In South Dakota there is a special mountain called Mount Rushmore. Years ago workers carved four men's heads into its rock. They had to blast and then chip the rock very carefully in order to form the faces. At one point they had to start all over again. Each head is 60 feet (20 m) tall! It took 14 years for workers to shape the heads. They are of George Washington, Thomas Jefferson, Abraham Lincoln, and Theodore Roosevelt. All of these men once served as U.S. presidents.

What is the main idea?

(a) In South Dakota there is a special mountain called Mount Rushmore.

(b) Each president's head is 60 feet tall.

(c) It took 14 years for workers to finish carving all four heads.

(d) George Washington, Thomas Jefferson, Abraham Lincoln, and Theodore Roosevelt are all former U.S. presidents.

Passage 6

One day, a man went to market to sell his grain. Onto the tiny donkey's back he loaded all sorts of bags and packages. The donkey had to carry all of the grain the farmer planned to sell, the food they would need on the journey, and gifts for his friends in town. The horse's job was only to carry his master. They started on their way to town, which was about three days' journey away.

Step by painful step, the donkey bore its heavy load. The sun beat down on her, and she felt exhausted. Soon her breathing became ragged. Just a short time later, the load completely overwhelmed her. She collapsed in the middle of the road. Although the donkey struggled to stand up, she could not do so.

What is the main idea?

(a) The horse is lazy and chooses to carry only the man.

(b) The overloaded donkey collapses on the way to town.

(c) A man is going to market to sell his grain.

(d) The donkey comes down with an illness on the way into town.

Passage 7

Today we get foods from all over the world, often within a matter of a few days. Think about kiwis. Most of these tasty fruits grow in New Zealand, yet you can buy them at your local store. How do they get there? Ships, planes, trains, and trucks transport them. In the case of kiwis, they leave their country on a ship or a plane. When they arrive in the U.S., the fruit gets unloaded and put onto a train. At the train station, a truck picks up the kiwis and drives them to your grocery store.

What is the main idea?

(a) Trains deliver fresh fruit to stores.

(b) Kiwis leave their country on a ship or plane.

(c) Trucks are important in moving food quickly.

(d) We can buy foods from all over the world in our grocery stores.

Passage 8

As soon as they were all hidden behind the shrubs, Sharon said, "I think we'd better call Dad as soon as . . ." She was interrupted by a sudden scream.

"What was that?" Sidney cried, looking terrified.

"It sounded like it came from inside that creepy old lodge," Elaine said, jumping up and stepping from behind the bush.

"Elaine!" Sharon cried in a whisper. "Where are you going? Don't tell me you intend to actually go inside!"

Elaine continued to creep toward the building, glancing back over her shoulder at her sisters. "Well, that's the only way we're going to find whoever screamed, isn't it?"

Just then they heard another scream. Chills ran down each girl's spine as all three looked in the direction the scream had come from.

"Somebody's in trouble!" Elaine cried. "We've got to help." She broke into a run.

What is the main idea?

(a) The girls are all too afraid to help whoever is screaming.

(b) Elaine gives away the girls' hiding spot.

(c) Elaine wants to help whoever is screaming.

(d) The girls all rush to help whoever is screaming.

Passage 9

The Inuit people live in small villages in Russia, Alaska, Canada, and Greenland. Many Inuit live in the same way as their ancestors. The women teach the girls to cook and sew. The men teach the boys how to fish and to hunt for moose and whale.

The Inuit have survived for thousands of years in some of the harshest, coldest places on Earth. They live by an important rule: each person does all he or she can to help the whole group to survive. For example, no matter who catches a whale, everyone shares the food and oil from it. This ensures that no one will go hungry.

What is the main idea?

(a) The men teach the boys how to fish and to hunt for moose and whale.

(b) Inuits have traditional roles for men and women.

(c) The Inuit people live in small villages in Russia, Alaska, Canada, and Greenland.

(d) The Inuits' tradition of sharing keeps them alive in a harsh climate.

Passage 10

The Grand Canyon in Arizona is one of the natural wonders of the world. The Canyon's rim towers over the Colorado River far below. This river has snaked through the Canyon for millions of years. During this time it has carved its way through many layers of rock. This left rock layers exposed. The different colors show the various types of rocks in each layer. The part closest to the river is black. The layer above it is a brilliant red. The next layer looks brown or light purple. It depends on how the sunlight hits it. The Grand Canyon has other layers, too. Its top layer is dull gray limestone.

What is the main idea?

(a) The Grand Canyon in Arizona is one of the natural wonders of the world.

(b) The Grand Canyon has many different rock layers.

(c) The top layer of the Grand Canyon is dull gray limestone.

(d) The Colorado River carved the Grand Canyon.

You can picture the main idea as a flag flying at the top of a pole. The flag is what you notice first. The flag is like the main idea. It's most important, just like the main idea. The flagpole holds up the flag, just as the details hold up, or support, the main idea.

Details:

☞ **give more facts about the main idea**

☞ **provide reasons**

☞ **show examples**

Passage 1

Skunks are fascinating animals that can live for ten years. Unlike their ferret cousins, skunks are always black and white. They eat insects, worms, snails, bees, and wasps. Each night they use their noses to seek food. They can even smell bugs hidden under the ground. Skunks try to avoid water. Yet they can swim—for hours if necessary. They can run up to 10 miles per hour (16 kph) for a short time. Skunks usually flee from an enemy. However, if a skunk gets cornered, it lifts its tail and sprays bad-smelling oil at its enemy's face.

Skunks live in North America, Central America, and parts of South America. During the summer they live in hollow trees or piles of hay. In places with cold winters, skunks dig burrows and hibernate. Sometimes they share these winter homes with raccoons or rabbits. While these may seem like strange bedfellows, the body heat of several animals keeps them all warmer.

The main idea is:

ⓐ Skunks are interesting animals that are well-equipped to survive.

ⓑ Although skunks, raccoons, and rabbits may seem like unlikely bedfellows, the body heat of several animals keeps them all warmer.

ⓒ Skunks live in North America, Central America, and parts of South America.

ⓓ Skunks have an amazing sense of smell.

The main idea is supported by these six details:

1. _____

2. _____

3. _____

4. _____

5. _____

6. _____

Passage 2

Emily looked down at the smashed vase in horror. Her mother's favorite vase—broken! The beautiful vase that had been her grandmother's lay shattered at her feet. Emily fought back tears as she gathered up the pieces. How on earth was she going to explain this?

The main idea is:

ⓐ The beautiful vase that had been her grandmother's lay shattered at her feet.

ⓑ Emily tries not to cry, even though she's afraid of getting into a lot of trouble.

ⓒ Emily gets upset when she breaks a vase that meant a lot to her mother and grandmother.

ⓓ Emily must think of an explanation for the broken vase.

The main idea is supported by these three details:

1. _____

2. _____

3. _____

Passage 3

Eating a balanced diet is important. To stay healthy, you need foods from each of the food groups. Different foods give your body the protein, vitamins, and minerals it needs. Fruits and vegetables give you fiber, minerals, and vitamins A and C. Foods made of grains give you energy. Eating meat, beans, and nuts sends protein to your skin, muscles, and bones. Calcium from milk and dairy products keeps your bones and teeth strong.

The main idea is:

ⓐ You get energy from foods made of grains.

ⓑ Eating a balanced diet is important.

ⓒ Your bones and teeth need calcium.

ⓓ Fruits and vegetables give you fiber, minerals, and vitamins A and C.

The main idea is supported by these four details:

1. _____

2. _____

3. _____

4. _____

Passage 4

The Apatosaurus was the largest animal to ever live on land. Its long neck had a tiny head perched on top. It also had a long tail, which it used as a whip when attacked. Due to its size, if it fell, it would have a hard time getting up again. So this dinosaur had five toes on each of its feet to help it stay upright. Since it was so big, when it walked, it moved very slowly. Apatosauruses roamed in herds, eating the leaves from the tops of trees. They could live for 100 years.

The main idea is:

ⓐ The Apatosaurus was so big that it walked slowly.

ⓑ The Apatosaurus could live for 100 years.

ⓒ The Apatosaurus had five toes so it would stay balanced and not fall down.

ⓓ The Apatosaurus was the largest animal to ever live on land.

The main idea is supported by these four details:

1. _____   3. _____

2. _____   4. _____

Passage 5

Mom turned the key in the lock and held the door open with her hip as she flipped the light switch on. Everyone gasped. Their kitchen looked as if an earthquake had struck it. Pots and pans littered the floor. The table lay on its side. Sharp pieces of plates and shattered drinking glasses lay everywhere. It appeared as if someone had torn open each cabinet and yanked everything onto the floor.

"What happened?" Randy was the first to find his voice.

"I think that our home's been broken into," his mother responded quietly.

"It looks like whoever did it wanted to wreck everything," said Betsy.

What is the main idea?

ⓐ Someone has broken into the people's home.

ⓑ Sharp pieces of plates and shattered drinking glasses lay everywhere.

ⓒ The kitchen looked as if an earthquake had struck it.

ⓓ It appeared as if someone had torn open each cabinet and yanked everything onto the floor.

The main idea is supported by these four details:

1. _____   3. _____

2. _____   4. _____

Passage 6

A vulture's head is well adapted to its needs. Vultures eat dead animals. This means that they must stick their heads into dead bodies. If they had feathers on their heads, they'd get blood all over them. So every year of their life vultures shed more of their head feathers. Over time they lose all the feathers on their heads and necks.

The main idea is:

ⓐ Vultures stick their heads inside the bodies of dead animals.

ⓑ Every year a vulture loses more of its head feathers.

ⓒ A vulture's head is well adapted to its needs.

ⓓ You can tell a vulture's age by the number of feathers on its head and neck.

The main idea is supported by these three details:

1. _____   3. _____

2. _____

Passage 7

During the Middle Ages (500 to 1500 A.D.) in Europe, there were no central governments. Instead, each lord owned a piece of land. These rich landowners built huge stone castles. They lived inside, and so did their knights. Knights protected the lord and his land. The peasants who worked the lord's fields lived outside of the castle in little huts.

Lords often went to war against each other. They wanted more land and more power. Such fighting injured or killed the peasants, trampled their crops, and killed their livestock. Only if the peasants made it to the castle before the drawbridge closed could they hide inside.

Many castles had water-filled moats around them. This kept enemies from getting too close. Heavy drawbridges could be lifted to keep invaders out. From the top of the walls, men shot arrows, threw rocks, and poured boiling water down onto attackers.

The main idea is:

ⓐ There were no central governments in Europe during the Middle Ages.

ⓑ During the Middle Ages, lords frequently attacked each other's castles.

ⓒ Castles had moats to keep enemies from getting too close to the walls.

ⓓ During the Middle Ages a lord's castle always gave protection to his peasants during an attack.

The main idea is supported by these four details:

1. _____   3. _____

2. _____   4. _____

Passage 8

When I arrived at Ur today, I felt overwhelmed by the city's size. Long before I reached the city, I saw its massive temple rising above everything. It towered over all the other buildings and seemed to dwarf the large wall that protected the city. It was very beautiful.

I'd never want to live here. It's not that I mind the crowds—although never have I seen so many people crammed into so little space. The streets are narrow and the houses small. But what really bothers me is the sewage and rotting food scraps lying in the streets. I much prefer my town of Cultha.

The main idea is:

   (a) The writer would rather live in Cultha than Ur.

   (b) The writer hates Ur because it's too big and crowded.

   (c) The writer didn't like the sewage and rotting food scraps in the streets.

   (d) The writer thought that Ur's temple was beautiful.

The main idea is supported by these four details:

1. _____   3. _____

2. _____   4. _____

Passage 9

Glaciers change the Earth's surface in many different ways. These slow-moving ice sheets form lakes by preventing water from draining away. Rivers change their courses to flow along the ice's edges. Rain or snow falls on the glaciers. When that water freezes, it adds weight, which can push the Earth's crust down. The freezing and thawing of glaciers causes rocks under and near the ice sheet to break off. These loose rock pieces get dragged along, scratching deep grooves into the land. This is how glaciers have turned some V-shaped mountain valleys into wider, deeper U-shaped valleys. As a glacier retreats, or melts, it drops pieces of rock and soil. This forms hills and ridges.

The main idea is:

   (a) As a glacier retreats, or melts, it drops pieces of rock and soil.

   (b) The freezing and thawing of glaciers causes rocks under the ice sheet to break off.

   (c) Glaciers change the Earth's surface in many different ways.

   (d) Rivers change their courses to flow along the glacier's edges.

The main idea is supported by these four details:

1. _____   3. _____

2. _____   4. _____

Passage 10

Life on a World War II submarine was tough. The air wasn't fresh. It got used over and over again. It was crowded, too. The only place to be alone was the bathroom. In the main aisle of the sub each person had to often pause while someone else squeezed past. Each person's bunk was just big enough to lie on. Serving on a sub was scary, too. If an enemy discovered a sub, the sailors had to shut down its engines and hope that the depth charges that the enemy fired on them would miss.

Due to these hardships, no one was assigned to a sub. Instead, everyone on a sub volunteered. Before going down, these men had to pass physical and mental testing. They had to convince doctors that they wouldn't crack under the pressure of being thousands of feet below water with almost no chance for escape or rescue.

The main idea is:

(a) Everyone on a World War II submarine was a volunteer.

(b) It was crowded on a World War II submarine.

(c) Serving on a World War II submarine was dangerous.

(d) Life on a World War II submarine was tough.

The main idea is supported by these six details.

1. _____   4. _____

2. _____   5. _____

3. _____   6. _____

Passage 11

Discarded furniture filled the small attic. A large oval mirror and several big black trunks stood near the one tiny window. Stacks of old magazines lined one wall. Everything was covered with a thick layer of dust. The only footprints belonged to Sue.

"There's nobody up here," Sue said. "And it doesn't look as if anyone's been up here in a very long time." She didn't know whether to be glad or not. "Let's check outdoors."

The main idea is:

(a) Everything was covered with a thick layer of dust.

(b) Sue didn't know whether to be glad or not.

(c) Nobody's been in the attic recently except for Sue.

(d) Discarded furniture filled the small attic.

The main idea is supported by these three details:

1. _____

2. _____

3. _____

You can find the main idea and supporting details by looking for the answers to these questions:

☞ **who or what**   ☞ **where**

☞ **did what**   ☞ **why**

☞ **when**   ☞ **how**

Passage 1

Valerie frantically pressed the numbers on the keypad. "It won't open, Mom!" she screamed, her mind clouded by pain and fear. Then she spied the 'execute' button and pressed it. The door swung open.

"Get inside the vault now! No matter what happens, don't open this door," cried Mom.

Valerie stumbled in, pulling Mark with her.

Glancing over her shoulder, she saw the heavy metal door swinging closed. She cried out, "Wait, Mom! Aren't you coming?" As the door crashed shut, the Earth shook like a rabbit cornered by a ferocious dog. Things crashed to the floor around the children. Valerie pulled Mark down to the floor, trying to cover him with her own body. She threw her hands over her head. The shaking and noise seemed to go on and on—but in reality it lasted only about a minute.

The moment the shaking stopped, silence filled her ears. It was unnaturally quiet; a silence like she'd never experienced before. Then she heard her little brother whimpering weakly. Valerie tried to force down a growing sense of terror. At least she had her brother to keep her company.

Find the answers in the passage. One of the questions is not answered.

Who or What?: _Valerie and Mark_

Did What?: _____

When?: _____

Where?: _____

Why?: _____

How?: _____

Passage 2

Gregor Mendel tended the gardens at the monastery where he and the other monks lived. He did experiments with pea plants for eight years. Around 1860 he proved that parents passed traits to their offspring. He found that plants have genes. Genes carry features from one generation to the next. He also discovered recessive and dominant genes. Dominant genes showed up the most often in offspring. Recessive genes only showed up occasionally, and only when both parents carried the gene for the trait.

How did he figure this out? He bred a tall pea plant with a short pea plant. Every one of the first generation of four pea plants was tall. This meant that tall was the dominant gene. Yet in the next generation of four pea plants, one plant was very short. It had gotten recessive short genes from both of its parent plants.

Find the answers in the passage.

Who or What?: _____

Did What?: _____

When?: _____

Where?: _____

Why?: _____

How?: _____ he did experiments on pea plants _____

Passage 3

Ted and David started searching the tall grass and weeds for building materials. They found several weathered wooden pallets that had been thrown in the field as trash. It took both boys to carry each one to the base of the tree. The pallets could form the floor and walls of their tree fort. The only problem was going to be getting them up the huge oak.

Find the answers in the passage. One of the questions is not answered.

Who or What?: _____

Did What?: _____

When?: _____

Where?: _____ in a field _____

Why?: _____

How?: _____

Passage 4

Lakesha came in and asked, "What are you doing in here, Tamika? Don't you want to play the Star Wars Monopoly game Marcus just got for Christmas?"

"Sure," I agreed and started down the stairs with her. "What's the Kwanzaa principle for tonight?"

"Cooperative economics," Lakesha said. She looked at me and saw that I had no idea what she meant.

"You know," she went on, "share what you have with others. When everyone gives a little, it adds up to a lot. If each person who knew a poor kid gave him just $10, he'd probably end up with $1,000." Lakesha laughed. "It's a good idea for real life, but I don't think you should try it during Monopoly if you want to win!"

Find the answers in the passage.

Who or What?: _____

Did What?: _____explained a Kwanzaa principle to Tamika_____

When?: _____

Where?: _____

Why?: _____

How?: _____

Passage 5

The Spanish explorer Ponce de Leon wanted to find the Fountain of Youth. He felt that if he bathed in its waters, he would never grow old. He also thought that he could sell the water for a lot of money to others who also didn't want to age. In 1513 he sailed to the New World. He landed on the Atlantic Coast and began his search. He named the area where he came ashore Florida. The name means "flowery" in Spanish. In Florida flowers bloom no matter what the season. That's because the sun shines an average of 220 days each year.

Ponce de Leon also searched the Bahamas and Puerto Rico. He looked for years, but never found the Fountain of Youth. It doesn't exist. But he did find a land which many people today call paradise. Florida has a warm climate, lots of sunshine, and beautiful flowers.

Find the answers in the passage.

Who or What?: _____

Did What?: _____looked for the Fountain of Youth_____

When?: _____

Where?: _____

Why?: _____

How?: _____

Passage 6

We would have little knowledge about Ancient Egypt without a stone that was found by accident. The Rosetta Stone unlocked much of Egypt's history.

In 1799 a French soldier tore down an old wall. The wall stood inside of a fort in Egypt. In the wall the soldier found an odd stone. The black slab had three languages carved on it. He showed it to his officer. The officer knew it was an important find. They carefully removed the stone from the wall. Then they turned the Rosetta Stone over to scholars.

Until that time no one knew how to read hieroglyphics, the language of ancient Egypt. They had been seen in different places all over Egypt, but nobody knew what they meant. The Rosetta Stone had the same message written in Greek and hieroglyphics. Many people knew Greek. They used their understanding of Greek to read the hieroglyphics. It took them 20 years before they understood all of the symbols. This let them figure out many other old Egyptian writings as well.

Find the answers in the passage. One of the questions is not answered.

Who or What?:_____

Did What?: _____

When?: _____

Where?: _____

Why?: _____

How?: _used their knowledge of Greek to decode the hieroglyphics on the Rosetta Stone_

Passage 7

The elf tapped carefully all around the edge of the great boulder. Suddenly he cried out, "I've found it!" He had discovered a tiny hidden latch on one side of the stone, no bigger than a thumb. When he pulled on it, the stone rolled inward. The elves held their torches high as they cautiously moved forward into the dark tunnel.

Find the answers in the passage. One of the questions is not answered.

Who or What?:_____

Did What?: _____

When?: _____

Where?: _____at the entrance to a tunnel_____

Why?: _____

How?: _____

Passage 8

In 1914 Garrett Morgan made the first gas mask. He called it a safety hood. Its tight canvas hood had a breathing tube that hung to the ground. The bottom of the tube was lined with a sponge-type material to help filter the air. Another tube allowed the wearer to exhale air out. This let a person breathe clean air even in the midst of deadly fumes. Morgan took his invention to several companies. Since he was black, no one showed any interest. Then, in 1916, an explosion in Cleveland, Ohio, showed how well his safety hood worked.

The explosion left workers trapped in a tunnel under the city. Although still alive, their situation looked grim. Smoke and natural gas fumes had killed the firemen who tried to reach them. No one knew a way to get the men out alive.

When Morgan heard about the accident, he and his brother rushed to the scene. They put on safety hoods and went down into the tunnel. They saved 32 men's lives. After the newspapers reported the story, orders poured in for Morgan's gas masks.

Find the answers in the passage.

Who or What?: _____

Did What?: ___rescued trapped workers_____

When?: _____

Where?: _____

Why?: _____

How?: _____

Passage 9

Colby bent down and picked up the bulging envelope. Someone had probably dropped it on the way to the post office. He turned it over, surprised to see a blank front. Colby wondered what he should do with the mysterious envelope. After all, it had no address or return address. He had no idea who it came from or where it was going.

Then he noticed the flap was loose. Not open, but barely sealed. Perhaps he could find out whom the envelope belonged to by looking inside. He broke the remaining seal and gasped. The envelope was full of money. Colby quickly began counting. There were 27 twenty-dollar bills. He counted again. There was no doubt about it—he had $540 in his hand.

Find the answers in the passage.

Who or What?: _____

Did What?: _____

When?: _____

Where?: _____

Why?: _____

How?: ___by breaking the seal on the envelope_____

Knowing these facts will help you locate topic sentences:

☞ A topic sentence states the main idea of a paragraph.

☞ Topic sentences are used often in nonfiction text.

☞ Usually topic sentences come at the start of a paragraph and are followed by details.

☞ Sometimes topic sentences fall in the middle of a paragraph. They are surrounded on both sides by details.

☞ Occasionally, topic sentences come at the end of a paragraph. They sum up the details that have come before.

Passage 1

About 400 years ago a settlement was formed in Jamestown, Virginia. Settlers from England arrived there and built a fort near the James River. They had a tough life. Many died fighting the Spanish and Native Americans. Even more died from disease. By 1699 no one lived at the fort. The people left no evidence or record of what occurred. It was as if they just vanished. No one knows exactly what happened to the people who lived in Jamestown.

A few years ago scientists unearthed the fort. They found guns, pots, coins, and toys. They hope that these things will help them to solve the mystery of what happened to the settlement at Jamestown. Even so, we may never know for certain.

What is the topic sentence?

(a) A few years ago scientists unearthed the fort.

(b) No one knows exactly what happened to the people who lived in Jamestown.

(c) The people left no evidence or record of what occurred.

(d) About 400 years ago a settlement was formed in Jamestown, Virginia.

Check one of the boxes to complete this sentence:

The topic sentence in this paragraph comes at the ❑ beginning ❑ middle ❑ end.

Passage 2

As they talked, the animals reluctantly agreed that they each should visit the sick King Lion. If they stayed away, he'd be mad and punish them after he got better. So one at a time, or in small groups, the animals went to the royal cave. Some gave him gifts, such as the best bit of meat from a recent catch. Others just went to ask about his health. Large and small, all of the animals in the kingdom visited the lion in his cave.

(a) Some gave him gifts, such as the best bit of meat from a recent catch.

(b) If they stayed away, he'd be mad and punish them after he got better.

(c) Large and small, all of the animals in the kingdom visited the lion in his cave.

(d) Others just went to ask about his health.

Check one of the boxes to complete this sentence:

The topic sentence in this paragraph comes at the ❑ beginning ❑ middle ❑ end.

Passage 3

The Wilson Estate was a large stone structure visible for miles around. Everyone in the area knew it by name. Since 1804 it had stood on a cliff overlooking the sea. The Estate looked as if it could withstand the very worst storm nature could throw at it. Two round towers marked each end of the building, making it look like a castle. All it lacked was a moat and drawbridge.

Check one of the boxes to complete this sentence:

The topic sentence in this paragraph comes at the ❑ beginning ❑ middle ❑ end.

What is the topic sentence?

ⓐ Since 1804 it had stood on a cliff overlooking the lake.

ⓑ All it lacked was a moat and drawbridge.

ⓒ Two round towers marked each end of the building, making it look like a castle.

ⓓ The Wilson Estate was a large stone structure visible for miles around.

Passage 4

Spanish men watched Native Americans in South America play ball games. They had balls made from the gum that oozed from trees. The Spanish men thought the gum was interesting. They called it "India rubber" and took it home. Nobody thought much of their discovery. No one saw a use for the gum.

Then a Scottish man named Charles Macintosh thought of a good use for India rubber. He put a thin coating on two pieces of cloth. Then he put the cloth pieces together with the rubber in the middle. The rubber stuck to itself like glue. This made the cloth waterproof. Never before had anyone made waterproof fabric. Whenever it rained, anyone who went outside got soaked.

Macintosh immediately saw a need for the new fabric. He used it to make a "macintosh," his word for raincoat. His coats were a big success. Although they are now made of plastic-coated fabric, people in England still call their raincoats macintoshes.

What is the topic sentence?

ⓐ Then a Scottish man named Charles Macintosh thought of a good use for India rubber.

ⓑ Spanish men watched Native Americans in South America play ball games.

ⓒ No one saw a use for the gum.

ⓓ Although they are now made of plastic-coated fabric, people in England still call their raincoats macintoshes.

Check one of the boxes to complete this sentence:

The topic sentence in this paragraph comes at the ❑ beginning ❑ middle ❑ end.

Passage 5

Cory squatted over the coffee can lying on its side in the field. His mother came up beside him.

"Look inside," Cory said eagerly. "There's something alive."

His mother, looking doubtful, peered into the can. Tiny black things moved around in the rainwater that had collected in the can.

"We should dump this," she said. "It's a breeding place for bugs. They're probably tiny mosquitoes."

"No, Mom, look closer," Cory insisted, gently poking at the can's inhabitants with a stick. One stuck to the stick as he pulled it out. It was clearly a tiny black tadpole. A toad had laid her eggs inside the coffee can.

What is the topic sentence?

(a) One stuck to the stick as he pulled it out.

(b) His mother, looking doubtful, peered into the can.

(c) A toad had laid her eggs inside the coffee can.

(d) Cory squatted over the coffee can lying on its side in the field.

Check one of the boxes to complete this sentence:

The topic sentence in this paragraph comes at the ❑ beginning ❑ middle ❑ end.

Passage 6

Sometimes volcanoes show up in odd places. One example occurred in Mexico. In February of 1943, earthquakes shook a farmer and his family. A few days later, the farmer saw steam rising from his cornfield. The next day the field had a wide crack. Smoke and ashes shot up out of the crack. A volcano was erupting right in the middle of his field! Over the next nine years, lava and ash formed a cone that rose more than a quarter mile high. In addition to ruining the farm, several nearby towns lay buried beneath lava. Then just as suddenly as it had started, it stopped.

What is the topic sentence?

(a) In February of 1943, earthquakes shook a farmer and his family.

(b) Sometimes volcanoes show up in odd places.

(c) Smoke and ashes shot up out of the crack.

(d) Then just as suddenly as it had started, it stopped.

Check one of the boxes to complete this sentence:

The topic sentence in this paragraph comes at the ❑ beginning ❑ middle ❑ end.

Passage 7

An old woman once owned a stubborn donkey. He would never do as he was told, and he delighted in being difficult. When the old woman who owned him wanted him to come out of the barn, he refused to leave his stall. When she tried to lead him into the barn, he wouldn't enter. If she wanted him to go to the right, he always pulled to the left. If she wanted him to go to the left, he would go to the right. The donkey always did the opposite of whatever the old woman said.

What is the topic sentence?

ⓐ The donkey always did the opposite of whatever the old woman said.

ⓑ When the old woman who owned him wanted him to come out of the barn, he refused to leave his stall.

ⓒ When she tried to lead him into the barn, he wouldn't enter.

ⓓ If she wanted him to go to the right, he always pulled to the left.

Check one of the boxes to complete this sentence:

The topic sentence in this paragraph comes at the ❑ beginning ❑ middle ❑ end.

Passage 8

The Empire State Building has been part of New York City for over 70 years. Built in 1931, it was the world's tallest building. It kept that title until 1973. Today it is one of the places that most New York visitors go.

Many interesting facts are known about this skyscraper. It gets hit by lightning about 24 times every year. People race to see who can reach the top of its 1,860 steps first each year. The yearly electric bill is over $3.5 million.

There are sad facts, too. In July of 1945, an Air Force jet got lost in the fog. It crashed into the Building. Fourteen people died.

During the 1930s, the Empire State Building's owners couldn't pay its taxes. They began charging people to go to the top. Many people paid the fee. They wanted to stand on the observation deck so high above the city. Enough money came in to pay the taxes.

What is the topic sentence?

ⓐ Today it is one of the places that most New York visitors go.

ⓑ Many interesting facts are known about this skyscraper.

ⓒ Enough money came in to pay the taxes.

ⓓ Built in 1931, it was the world's tallest building.

Check one of the boxes to complete this sentence:

The topic sentence in this paragraph comes at the ❑ beginning ❑ middle ❑ end.

Passage 9

Kelly hated going to the doctor's office. She hoped this wasn't one of those visits where she'd have to get a shot. It seemed like every time she went in for a checkup, she needed a shot. Even worse, the nurse sometimes pricked her finger and took blood. Kelly shuddered and wished that it was tomorrow. She wished the visit was already a memory.

What is the topic sentence?

ⓐ Even worse, the nurse sometimes pricked her finger and took blood.

ⓑ It seemed like every time she went in for a checkup, Kelly needed a shot.

ⓒ She hoped this wasn't one of those visits where she'd have to get a shot.

ⓓ Kelly hated going to the doctor's office.

Check one of the boxes to complete this sentence:

The topic sentence in this paragraph comes at the ❏ beginning ❏ middle ❏ end.

Passage 10

You may have noticed the black lines of a bar code on the things you buy. Years ago nothing had bar codes. Prices were marked on each package. This took time, and people made errors. This method also didn't give the stores detailed information.

To succeed, stores must know which items sell and which ones don't. Then managers can reorder or discontinue products. Bar codes, or UPCs, (Uniform Pricing Code) help stores keep track of sales. When an item gets scanned at the checkout, the code tells the product's size, description, and maker. These details are recorded within computerized cash registers.

To buy an item, the UPC is passed over a laser beam. The laser shines on the bar code and rapidly matches it to a list of items in the computer. This makes going through checkout fast and accurate. It limits human error. However, mistakes can still be made. For example, if an item is on sale but the change to its price isn't made in the computer, the customer will get charged the wrong amount.

What is the topic sentence?

ⓐ If an item is on sale but the change to its price isn't made in the computer, the customer will get charged the wrong amount.

ⓑ You may have noticed the black lines of a bar code on the things you buy.

ⓒ To succeed, stores must know which items sell and which ones don't.

ⓓ Bar codes, or UPCs, help stores keep track of sales.

Check one of the boxes to complete this sentence:

The topic sentence in this paragraph comes at the ❏ beginning ❏ middle ❏ end.

Passage 11

One day, a man with three grown sons built a new cabin at the edge of his land. It had just one room and no windows, but each of the sons wanted it for his own. The father said that whomever could fill the home completely—including every corner—would earn it as a prize. The oldest son tried filling the place with cows, but he found that a lot of space remained around their bodies. The middle son tried to fill the cabin with hay, but he failed, too. Then the youngest son brought a candle into the home. When he lit it, light filled every part of the cabin. The father gave the youngest son the cabin.

What is the topic sentence?

(a) One day, a man with three grown sons built a new cabin at the edge of his land.

(b) The father said that whomever could fill the home completely—even in every corner— would earn it as a prize.

(c) The father gave the youngest son the cabin.

(d) It had just one room and no windows, but each of the sons wanted it for his own.

Check one of the boxes to complete this sentence:

The topic sentence in this paragraph comes at the ❑ beginning ❑ middle ❑ end.

Passage 12

Yellowstone National Park sits above one of the Earth's "hot spots." A hot spot is a place where the molten rock from the center of the Earth is within four miles of the surface. The heat turns ground water into steam. This hot water and steam blows up through holes in the ground. The places where this happens are called *geysers*. Most geysers aren't predictable. They may explode every couple of days or after dozens of years. However, one Yellowstone geyser, Old Faithful, erupts every 40 to 70 minutes, day in and day out. It has done so for hundreds of years.

In a hot spot, the Earth's crust rises and falls. For 60 years, Yellowstone rose a little more than half an inch a year. Since 1985 it has fallen at a rate of half an inch a year.

What is the topic sentence?

(a) In a hot spot the Earth's crust rises and falls.

(b) Most geysers aren't predictable.

(c) Yellowstone National Park sits above one of the Earth's "hot spots."

(d) Since 1985 it has fallen at a rate of half an inch a year.

Check one of the boxes to complete this sentence:

The topic sentence in this paragraph comes at the ❑ beginning ❑ middle ❑ end.

The main idea is not always stated. This is often true in fiction. One way to figure out an unstated main idea is to make a "movie in your mind."

If the main idea is unstated in nonfiction, get the details by asking questions (see p. 16). Use the answers to piece together the main idea.

Passage 1

Mama bluejay and her babies lived in a nest. All the babies knew how to fly except one. No matter how hard Benjy tried, he just couldn't fly.

One day all of the other baby bluejays flew off for a day of fun. Benjy's mama tried to show him once again how to fly. All of a sudden she wobbled and fell over into the nest. Her eyes were closed, and she looked dead. Terrified, Benjy checked her and found her still breathing. After he tried to awaken her without success, he knew he must get help. If he waited for his brothers and sisters to get home, it might be too late. Closing his eyes, Benjy jumped from the edge of the nest. He landed with a thump on the ground. He began to hop along, cheeping loudly for help.

What is the main idea?

ⓐ Benjy Bluejay has a hard time learning how to fly.

ⓑ Mama Bluejay patiently tries to teach Benjy how to fly.

ⓒ Benjy leaves the nest to find help for his sick mama.

ⓓ All of Benjy's brothers and sisters have flown away for the day.

Passage 2

Have you ever wondered how the 50 states got their names? Many are those the Native Americans gave to the area. Hawaii is the word for "homeland." Missouri means "river of the big canoes." Michigan means "great water." Ohio means "good river."

Other states' names are based on the English language. Indiana stands for "land of Indians." King George named Georgia. Maine is short for "mainland." New Hampshire was named for a settler's home in England.

The reasons behind some names aren't as clear. Rhode Island was named for a Greek island. Texas means "friends" in Mexican. California was named after a made-up place in a story.

What is the main idea?

ⓐ The reasons behind some states' names aren't clear.

ⓑ Almost every state was named by Native Americans.

ⓒ You can see the English influence in most of the states' names.

ⓓ States' names come from Native American words, English words, and other sources.

Passage 3

The Tyrannosaurus Rex is probably the best-known dinosaur in the world. It had two tiny front paws that it used like hands. It stood on its two large hind legs most of the time. This meant that it walked in a manner similar to us. This huge meat eater could run up to 22 miles per hour. When it went after another dinosaur, there was almost no hope of escape. It hunted alone and grabbed its prey with sharp, jagged teeth. Thank goodness these animals have been extinct for millions of years! No one would be safe with Tyrannosaurus Rex around.

What is the main idea?

ⓐ Tyrannosaurus Rex is a well-known meat-eating dinosaur.

ⓑ Everyone is afraid of Tyrannosaurus Rex.

ⓒ The Tyrannosaurus Rex ate meat.

ⓓ Other dinosaurs tried to avoid the Tyrannosaurus Rex.

Passage 4

It was a warm night for the end of October, so the trick-or-treaters didn't have to wear jackets over their outfits. Dressed in her angel costume, Sofia skipped from door to door. She wanted to go to each house on the street.

One house near the end of the block had its front door standing open with the screen door shut. Light spilled from within. Sofia rang the bell and waited on the steps. A large black dog raced up the screen door, barking loudly. A young woman appeared and pushed the dog away. She opened the door just far enough to offer a basketful of candy to Sofia. As Sofia reached into the basket, she was knocked flat on the ground. The dog stood on all fours over her, barking. Sofia screamed.

What is the main idea?

ⓐ While out trick-or-treating, Sofia is terrified when a dog leaps on top of her.

ⓑ Sofia is greedy because she wants to get candy from every house on her street.

ⓒ Sofia gets candy at a house with a dog.

ⓓ Sofia enjoys wearing her angel costume on Halloween.

Passage 5

It was so boring riding in the wagon day after day. Tall grass waved in the breeze for as far as the eye could see in all directions. One day slid into another, but they all seemed the same. Sometimes Frank walked to give the oxen less weight to pull. Walking was boring and tiring. He'd almost welcome the wolf attacks and wildfires they'd been warned could happen. At least it would be something different. Maybe they were just going around and around in a huge circle. There just couldn't be this much grass in the whole world.

What is the main idea?

ⓐ Frank is seeing a lot of grass.

ⓑ Frank wishes he had something more interesting to do.

ⓒ Frank hopes that a pack of wolves will attack his wagon.

ⓓ Frank is tired of traveling across the prairie in a wagon.

Passage 6

The lion neared the place where the planes came and went. All of the animals must have heard him coming. The lion felt hungry and discouraged. "I'm hungry!" roared the lion.

From inside a plane came a monkey's voice, "Set me free, and I will show you lots of food."

The lion's empty stomach made him unable to resist. He leaped up into a hole in the airplane, landing in the cargo hold. It took a full minute before the lion could see what surrounded him. The cargo hold held crates and cages filled with different kinds of animals.

"I see what you mean about a feast," the lion said, smacking his lips.

"Actually we're not what I had in mind," said the monkey. "Please get me out of this cage. Then I will show you lots of food."

What is the main idea?

ⓐ A monkey calls out to a lion.

ⓑ When he is offered food, a lion jumps inside of a plane.

ⓒ When a lion jumps into a plane's cargo hold, he starts eating all of the animals.

ⓓ A lion goes out in search of some fun.

Passage 7

When the darkness cleared, I found that I was caught in a mass of wooden boards, broken bricks, mangled pieces of metal, and a dead cow. I still held Ana's limp body in my arms. I gave her a little shake, but she didn't respond. I struggled to free myself enough to put my hand in front of her nose and mouth. I felt warm breath. Ana and I had survived! We just had to get free from this mess.

I began screaming for help. Surely someone would hear me and help us. Then I thought about the wall of water that had roared through our valley, smashing and destroying and sweeping away everything in its path. Perhaps all of the other Johnstown citizens were also buried in this mess. Maybe there was nobody to save us. Maybe Ana and I were the only ones alive.

What is the main idea?

  (a) Due to a flood, the writer and Ana are trapped.

  (b) No one can hear the writer's screams for help.

  (c) After a fire, the writer and Ana are trapped.

  (d) The writer and Ana are trapped after a tornado strikes their town.

Passage 8

Today, ships must have enough lifeboats for everyone. Drills are held so that everyone knows what to do in an emergency. Air patrols warn ships of icebergs. These measures are taken to prevent a tragedy like the one that happened nearly 100 years ago.

In 1912 the *Titanic* set out on its first trip from England to New York City. The ship had over 2,200 people on board. But it only had enough lifeboats to hold half of them.

Near midnight on April 14 the *Titanic* hit an iceberg. It started to sink. The captain told his crew to radio for help and fill the lifeboats. Women and children got in the lifeboats. Men had to stay on board. At 2:20 a.m. the ship slid under the sea's dark surface. About two hours later another ship came and rescued the 706 survivors. Fewer than half of the people who started out reached New York City.

What is the main idea?

  (a) The *Titanic's* captain wasn't fit to pilot the ship.

  (b) Ship travel was made safer due to the *Titanic* tragedy.

  (c) There weren't enough lifeboats on the *Titanic*.

  (d) The *Titanic* hit an iceberg and sank.

Passage 9

Last week my family and I went to the local state park. Standing on the beach, we threw rocks into the lake. Each of us counted how many times our stones skipped (struck the water and bounced off). After a few bad tosses, I felt frustrated, so I went in search of the perfect stone. As I combed the stony shore, I saw my dad throw a rock that skipped ten times. Someday I'll do as well, I thought.

After what felt like a long search, I found a smooth, flat rock with rounded corners. It looked like the right kind of stone to go a long way. I took a throwing stance, flicked my wrist, and flung the stone. I held my breath, afraid that it would plummet the moment it hit the water. Instead it shot across the surface with lightning speed. It bounced eleven times! I'd done even better than my dad! I may never be able to do it again...but at least I did it once.

What is the main idea?

(a) Everyone in the writer's family is good at skipping rocks.

(b) The writer's family enjoys skipping stones at a state park.

(c) The writer is excited about having skipped a stone 11 times.

(d) The writer doubts he or she will ever repeat this performance.

Passage 10

That night around midnight, Jana awoke when she heard a sound below her window. She sat up in bed, listening. It sounded like someone was on the front porch. She got out of bed and went to her window. It looked down onto the porch roof, so she couldn't see anything.

"Hey!" Jana called out, throwing open the window and trying to sound gruff. "What's going on?"

Suddenly her eyes saw movement on the sidewalk as someone swung onto a bicycle. It wobbled for a moment. Then the rider sped off into the darkness.

Jana raced downstairs to the front door and onto the porch. She rushed down the sidewalk, eager to get a better look at whoever had just been on their front porch. Although she strained her eyes, the night had no moon, and she saw no sign of the mysterious rider.

What is the main idea?

(a) A person sneaks into Jana's room, wakes her up, and then escapes on a bicycle.

(b) Jana is rudely awakened by a person on a bike.

(c) The night is dark and moonless, so Jana can't see who woke her up.

(d) During the night Jana hears someone on her porch, but the person escapes.

Passage 11

An American art form began in 1938. That's when the first comic book starring Superman came out. The Man of Steel was a superhero. He came from the planet Krypton. Kids and adults both enjoyed these comic books. They liked the fact that the good guy always won. The books sold well. Soon Batman and Robin had their own series. They had a secret place called the Bat Cave and drove around in a Batmobile.

Over time Marvel Comics came up with more superheroes. They launched Spiderman and X-Men. These characters were popular. Toys, games, and clothing featured them. Now all of these comic book characters have had their own movies. Many have amusement rides—often roller coasters—named after them. Almost everyone in the U.S.A. knows their names.

What is the main idea?
- (a) In comic books, the superhero always wins.
- (b) Superman was the first comic book superhero.
- (c) Over time comic book superheroes have gained in number and popularity.
- (d) Some toys, games, and amusement rides are based on comic book superheroes.

Passage 12

Boiling clouds blotted out the sun. I knew we were in trouble. As the sky continued to darken, fear stabbed my heart. Bolts of lightning shot from the clouds down to earth, shaking the ground around us. Within minutes the skies opened, and rain poured down. We were soon ankle-deep in mud, and our wagon sank into the soft soil.

The wagon train leader decided we had to camp here tonight. Of course building a fire was out of the question; all of the grass and buffalo chips were drenched. We all took cover inside our own wagons. Our wagon was particularly crowded with 12 people and all of our remaining possessions. Since we barely had breathing room, my father put the food bags under the wagon. What a bad decision! During the night wild animals came and ripped open every single bag. In addition, I didn't get a wink of sleep pressed up against my brothers' wet, clammy bodies.

What is the main idea?
- (a) Wild animals eat the people's food when they leave the food bags under their wagon.
- (b) The people in a wagon train spend a miserable, wet night in a rainstorm.
- (c) The people inside the wagon can't sleep because it's too crowded.
- (d) The people can't build a fire in the rain because everything is wet.

Choosing the Best Title

To select a title, first decide what the main idea is. Then check your choices to see which one best fits the topic.

Passage 1

"My poor daisies!" wailed Irene. "They looked so pretty last night. Now they look dead." Irene took them to Jack's bedroom. Her big brother Jack knew everything. She held the vase of wilted daisies out to him and asked, "What killed my flowers?"

"Why, they're not dead," her brother looked up from his homework and declared. "They're just exhausted. They all went out last night and danced until dawn. Now they're so tired they're hanging their heads."

"But flowers don't dance," said Irene.

"Sure they do," Jack insisted. "When it's dark out and we're all asleep, every flower dances with the night fairies."

Irene wasn't sure that Jack was telling her the truth. "Have you ever seen the flowers dancing?" she demanded.

"No, of course not," Jack replied. "No one can watch the dances done by flowers and night fairies. Their dances are secret. Nobody can see them."

"Why can't we set up a video camera and tape them dancing?" Irene asked.

"Because no one knows exactly where these dances take place," Jack responded.

What is the best title for this passage?
(a) The Dancing Flowers
(b) Jack and Irene
(c) The Dancing Flowers and Fairies Videotape
(d) The Flower Contest

Passage 2

Every continent except for Antarctica has some grasslands. Grasslands are just what their name says: land covered by grass. They account for one-fourth of the Earth's land surface. Few trees grow there. Grasslands are usually found on flat ground far inland, away from large bodies of water. They often lie between deserts and forests. All over the world many farmers grow crops on grasslands.

What is the best title for this passage?
(a) Earth's Grass
(b) On Flat Ground
(c) All But Antarctica
(d) Grasslands

Passage 3

Chipmunks are small rodents that live in Asia and North America. Their small bodies are covered by light brown fur. Down their backs and tails, chipmunks have a white stripe bordered on both sides by black. Chipmunks scurry around, looking for seeds and nuts. When they find a piece of food, they hold it in their tiny front paws and chew it with their sharp teeth. They store extra food in their underground homes. Chipmunks hibernate through the winter. However, they wake up often, eat some stored food, and go back to sleep. If a hawk or owl doesn't catch a chipmunk, it can live to be three years old.

What is the best title for this passage?

(a) Chipmunks Make Good Pets

(b) Sleepy Chipmunks

(c) All About Chipmunks

(d) Storing Food for the Winter

Passage 4

Volcanoes constantly spill lava onto the sea floor. Water cools the lava into rock. Over time, the lava builds up. When the lava layers reach the sea's surface, an island forms. The world's newest island, Surtsey, appeared in 1963. Surtsey is 20 miles (33 km) south of Iceland. Workers on a fishing boat actually saw it happen. They saw clouds of smoke and steam rising in the distance. Out of curiosity, they went closer. The men watched as land broke through the sea's surface. The volcano kept erupting for three and a half years. Surtsey got bigger every day. When the lava stopped flowing, it was a mile wide.

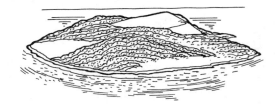

Near Hawaii, another volcano is now forming the island of Loihi. It currently lies a half mile below the sea's surface. It will probably be the Earth's next new island. Even so, thousands of years may pass before it rises above the water.

What is the best title for this passage?

(a) The Island of Surtsey

(b) Birth of a Volcano

(c) Underwater Volcanoes Make New Land

(d) Loihi's Volcano

Passage 5

When the light turned green, the twins stepped into the street. At the same time a girl on a skateboard kicked off toward them from the opposite side of the street. Within seconds a green van, with its horn blaring, ran the red light and sped into the intersection. It roared directly toward the twins. They jumped backwards. Tara tumbled and fell at the curb, landing hard on the sidewalk. She and Tory watched with horror as the van swerved toward the skateboarder.

To avoid a collision, the girl on the skateboard turned hard to the left. She smashed into the curb and flew off the board. She threw out her hands to break the fall. The van continued on its wild path just a little further until it slammed into a fire hydrant and came to a halt.

What is the best title for this passage?

   (a) A Scare at the Intersection

   (b) Skateboarding

   (c) The Twins Meet a Skateboarder

   (d) A Big Fall

Passage 6

A pond is a body of water that stays calm and still. It often freezes over during the winter. At the end of winter, a pond comes to life. Yellow flag iris and spring lilac are some of the first blossoms of spring. Although the cattails that line the pond's edges don't bloom, their green stalks add beauty and color to the landscape.

As the sun's warmth spreads throughout the water, animals start to stir at the pond's muddy bottom. Then fish, toads, frogs, and salamanders lay millions of eggs in the water. Before long, the pond is full of life. Newborn insects, snails, tadpoles, and tiny fish swim through the water or hide in the cattails. Snakes skim across the surface of the water, looking for a meal.

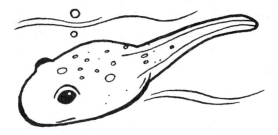

What is the best title for this passage?

   (a) Underwater Creatures

   (b) Spring Arrives at the Pond

   (c) The Life Cycle of a Pond

   (d) Endangered Pond Animals

Passage 7

As Ron swept his flashlight's beam over the building's brick facade, he spied a faint rectangular shape on the wall. "Look over here," he whispered excitedly to his friends.

The boys moved closer and saw a door so well concealed that it wouldn't have been visible even in broad daylight unless one was looking for it. In front of the secret door stood a screen of bushes. Nate tugged on the branches and found that they were fake.

"These were just put here to hide the door," he said. "We can move them aside without any trouble at all."

"This doorway explains a lot," Ron said. "Obviously the ghost must have gone through it. To us, it looked as though it walked right through the side of the building."

"I want to find out where it goes," stated Dan. "But I can't seem to find any way to open it."

What is the best title for this passage?
- (a) Search for the Ghost
- (b) The Friends Investigate
- (c) The Ghost Behind the Bushes
- (d) A Hidden Door

Passage 8

Scientists keep track of the Earth's atmosphere. In the mid-1970s they found a problem. The top layer of air, called the ozone layer, was getting too thin. In some places there were actually holes in this layer. This meant that there was less ozone. The ozone layer keeps harmful kinds of sun rays from reaching the Earth. These rays can hurt the skin of people and animals.

Scientists wanted to know what caused these holes. Over time, they found out that CFCs from spray cans, air conditioners, and refrigerators were the cause. The scientists told the world about the problem. It took a lot of time to convince people how important the problem was. Finally, by the mid-1990s, companies around the world had stopped putting CFCs in their products.

What is the best title for this passage?
- (a) Growing Holes in the Ozone Layer
- (b) CFCs Continue to Hurt the Ozone Layer
- (c) Protecting the Ozone Layer
- (d) The Earth's Atmosphere

Passage 9

One sunny day in early spring, the farmer surprised his family by saying, "Let's break some new ground today. I believe that there is better soil further down the valley."

The farmer, his wife, and their children walked until they reached a level piece of ground with dark, rich soil. They set to work. While the parents turned the sod, the children removed stones, carrying them to the far edge of the field. They all worked as hard as they could until dusk. Then they returned to their shabby little home. Although they were tired, they felt pleased at what they had accomplished. They felt sure that any crop planted in the new field would do well.

When they returned the next morning, they were shocked to find the field just as it had been when they first came upon it! All of the rocks they had removed were back in place. All of the sod they had turned the day before had been returned to its original position.

What is the best title for this passage?

(a) Turning Over New Soil

(b) The Mysterious Field

(c) Finding a New Field

(d) The Farmer and His Family

Passage 10

Miles below its surface, Earth has hot, melted rock. Directly above this melted rock is a layer of hot solid rocks. In some places this heated layer is close to the surface. People have found out how to use it to make electrical power. They use geothermal energy. *Geo* stands for Earth and *thermal* stands for heat. This energy does not pollute the environment, and it will never run out.

In 1904, Italians built the first geothermal power station. They found a place where steam rose from the ground. They trapped this steam and sent it through pipes to turbines. The turbines spun, making electricity.

In most places, steam does not come up on its own. So people pump water down to the hot rocks. About two-thirds of the water flows out into cracks in the rocks. The other one-third returns as steam. The steam drives turbines, which makes electricity.

The method isn't perfect. The steam brings up minerals that can harm the turbines. Still, most of Iceland's electricity is made this way. People hope to find more places and better ways to harness geothermal power.

What is the best title for this passage?

(a) Making Power from Earth's Heat

(b) Using Steam Turbines

(c) Making Electricity the Hard Way

(d) Italians Build First Geothermal Power Station

In order to summarize the main idea, follow these steps:

    Step 1: Look for the important words in the passage.

    Step 2: Identify how the important words relate to each other.

    Step 3: Based on Steps 1 & 2, write a sentence about the main idea.

Passage 1

Each bird wanted the large, beautiful rose for itself. They decided to give it as a prize to the most beautiful of them all. They asked a rabbit, a woodchuck, and a porcupine to act as judges and decide which bird deserved the lovely flower. One by one each of the birds flew before the animals. The judges looked at robins, blue jays, doves, and crows. They saw eagles, ducks, owls, and many more. The judges found it very hard to choose among so many pretty birds.

    Step 1: Underline the important words in the passage above.

    Step 2: What do these important words have in common?

    Step 3: Write a sentence stating the main idea:

_____

_____

Passage 2

Redwood trees have valuable lumber. In addition to its light red color, it has special qualities. It does not burn easily. Bugs don't eat it. Unlike most woods, it won't rot when exposed to weather. Since redwood is so desirable, lumber companies have cut many trees down. Few of these trees remain. Lumber companies own the land on which most of these remaining trees stand. Julia Hill wanted to save the redwoods. So she climbed up into the branches of one of these giants. She lived up there for two years. Hill refused to come down until the lumber company agreed to stop cutting down the trees.

    Step 1: Underline the important words in the passage above.

    Step 2: What do these important words have in common?

    Step 3: Write a sentence stating the main idea

_____

_____

Passage 3

Clad in a lifejacket, Cody waited on the dock, watching as the ski boat roared toward him. The instructor had told him that when the boat came up, he should grab onto the side rail that extended from its edge. He looked at the skis strapped to his feet. As he'd been instructed, he held them in the water, tips up. Cody swallowed. He felt both excited and afraid. He had dreamed of the moment when he would learn to water ski. Now that the time had come, he hoped it was as great as he'd imagined.

Step 1: Underline the important words in the passage above.

Step 2: What do these important words have in common?

Step 3: Write a sentence stating the main idea

_____

_____

Passage 4

When you want to heat food quickly, you put it in a microwave oven. It warms food faster than any stove, oven, toaster, or grill. Heating the air around the food makes these things cook more slowly. Microwaves don't heat the surrounding air.

Inside a microwave oven is a tube called a *magnetron*. It sends out radio waves. These waves make food atoms move back and forth very fast. They move billions of times each second. These moving atoms release energy, or heat. As the food heats from within, none of the energy gets lost. Microwaves also do not waste energy heating plates or bowls.

Microwave cookware is made of glass, china, and some kinds of plastic. These materials do not respond to the microwaves. So why do you need a potholder to take a bowl out of the microwave? The bowl absorbed heat from the food within it.

Step 1: Underline the important words in the passage above.

Step 2: What do these important words have in common?

Step 3: Write a sentence stating the main idea:

_____

_____

Passage 5

Once a little boy moved from the city to the country. His parents felt happy to escape from the crowds and congestion, but the boy found the country too quiet. When they had lived in an apartment building, cars drove by his windows all night long. Trains rumbled on the railroad tracks, and big planes flew overhead. But now in their snug little farmhouse there were no noises at night. Because the boy had lived with the noises all his life, he actually missed the night sounds. In the country he found it too silent to sleep!

Night after night he struggled to fall asleep. Even after he fell asleep, he often awoke after only an hour or two. He felt grumpy and tired every day. Then one night after he turned out his light and crawled into bed, he heard a noise. The sound was more beautiful than the engines of cars or planes or the clickety-clack of a train. It was a sweet humming, constant and steady. In a short while, the little boy fell sound asleep.

Write a sentence stating the main idea:

_____

_____

Passage 6

A boy made one of the best archaeological finds ever. He accidentally found the Dead Sea Scrolls in 1947. The boy had gone in search of his lost goat. He saw a small opening in the side of a cliff and idly threw a stone inside. He heard the sound of something breaking. He wondered if treasure lay inside the cave. Two days later the boy squeezed into the cave. There he found several large stone jars. They held two very old scrolls of parchment wrapped in linen and leather. The boy took them down the mountain. An archbishop in Jerusalem bought them.

Scholars looked at these scrolls. They realized that they were about 2,100 years old. This made them 1,000 years older than any other known Biblical manuscripts. The Dead Sea Scrolls made front-page news around the world.

The people living in the area looked for more scrolls. In 1952 they found more scrolls less than a mile from the first site. Pieces of 400 scrolls with parts of nearly every book of the Old Testament have been retrieved. Archaeologists know that an ancient group of Jewish monks lived in the area. For some unknown reason, they wrote the scrolls and hid them.

Write a sentence stating the main idea:

_____

_____

Passage 7

Kevin kept his eyes glued to the trail his dad had taken up the mountain, wishing he would appear. His father had promised not to go to the summit without Kevin. He said that he was just going to scout ahead and get their bearings. But he had been gone far too long. Scouting around should have taken him no more than half an hour at the most.

Kevin licked his lips nervously. He had promised his father that he'd stay put, but should he keep that promise? What if his dad was in trouble? Had he gotten hurt and was lying somewhere in pain, hoping Kevin would find him? Or was this just another one of his father's empty promises? Perhaps he didn't believe that Kevin could climb the ropes at the end of the trail to reach the summit. Maybe he'd gone to the summit alone and when he returned, he'd tell his son that the trail looked way too dangerous for them to continue. Kevin didn't know what to think.

Write a sentence stating the main idea:

_____

_____

Passage 8

The American bald eagle is the U.S.A.'s national bird. Congress chose it in 1782. They liked the bird's strength and beauty. They also chose the bald eagle because it is found only in North America and can live up to 50 years.

Most bald eagles choose a mate for life. They build a nest and lay just one or two eggs. After the eggs hatch, the parents take turns finding food for the babies. Salmon and other fish are their favorite food. The next year they use the same nest.

Just a few years ago, the number of American bald eagles was dropping. People got worried. Nobody wanted the national bird to die off completely. So steps have been taken to protect these magnificent birds. Now their numbers are rising again.

Write a sentence stating the main idea:

_____

_____

Passage 9

Jagged rocks lay at the base of the cliff, partially covered with water. Several of them jutted above the water, like a row of hideous black teeth. They glistened in the sunlight. This must be the dangerous reef the mysterious old captain had warned them about.

Their sailboat was heading right for the rocks. Every girl on board held her breath. With this wind, it seemed impossible that Lynn could steer the boat skillfully enough to avoid the rocks completely. Any one of them could rip a gash in the boat that would wreck it. They were still far enough off shore that it would be a long, cold swim to safety.

Write a sentence stating the main idea:

_____

_____

Passage 10

An avalanche happens when snow high up on a mountain starts to slide. As it slides, it knocks tons of snow loose. That snow also falls down the mountain. The wall of snow can move up to 100 miles per hour (160 kph). It can knock down full-grown trees. Some avalanches have buried whole towns.

Often people get buried under the snow. They may get so confused that they don't know which way to dig to reach the surface. They will run out of air if they don't get out from under the snow rapidly.

Many people think that St. Bernard dogs find the people who get caught in avalanches. Actually, German shepherds, border collies, and Labrador retrievers do the searching. With their keen sense of smell, dogs can rapidly check a snow-covered area. Once the dogs find the area, rescuers use long poles, called avalanche probes, to find the person's exact location. Then they dig as fast as they can. Every second counts.

After the victim is out, a helicopter takes him or her to a hospital. The helicopter crew sends down a long rope with a basket on the end. Rescuers strap the person into the basket, which the crew pulls back up. This method has increased the avalanche survival rate. The faster the victim gets warmth and oxygen, the more apt he or she is to live.

Write a sentence stating the main idea:

_____

_____

Passage 11

Mischief's stomach told him that Mr. McEntee was late bringing him lunch. When he finally came, he carried a cooler. Several other workers from his lab were with him. Mischief rubbed up against Mr. McEntee's leg. He said, "Come on, Mischief, let's have lunch at the seashore today." Mischief followed them to a nice place on the beach.

As he enjoyed a delicious can of tuna, Mischief noticed a small boat coming closer. It kept roaring towards them until it came right up onto the beach. Men jumped out. They carried guns and bags. Mischief quickly hid behind Mr. McEntee. The men pointed their guns at Mr. McEntee and his friends, and snarled, "Give us your uniforms!"

Write a sentence stating the main idea:

_____

_____

_____

Passage 12

Have you ever wondered how laundry detergent gets your clothes clean? Some of the chemicals in laundry soap let water enter cloth fibers more easily. Other chemicals lift the dirt. You can picture a molecule of laundry soap as a kite. The kite likes water. Its tail doesn't. In the washer the kites' tails are drawn to the grease, oil, and dirt on fabric. The tails attach themselves to the dirt. Meanwhile the kites themselves are attracted to the water. Just as a real kite rises into the air, the "soap kite" pulls its tail and the dirt attached to it out into the water. The tail releases the dirt from the cloth and leaves it in the wash water.

Another kind of soap uses enzymes. Enzymes are proteins produced by plants and animals. Soap enzymes cause a chemical break down of protein stains like grass, blood, gravy, and sweat. These stains should be treated first before the clothing goes into the water to give the enzymes time to work. Most laundry soaps include both kinds of cleaners to ensure your whole wash gets clean.

Write a sentence stating the main idea:

_____

_____

_____

Passage 1

In the late 1700s people often died if they caught smallpox. Jenner noticed that the girls who milked cows (milkmaids) almost never got smallpox. One day he asked a milkmaid about it. She said, "I can't get smallpox because I've had cowpox. Most of us milkmaids have caught it from our cows." This seemed to prove that cowpox and smallpox germs were similar. But how could this information be used to help people with smallpox? Jenner couldn't think of a way.

A few years later Jenner became a doctor. He found that his patients died of smallpox no matter what he did. He realized it was best to keep people from getting smallpox in the first place. Then Jenner had an idea. Cowpox, like chicken pox, made a person ill. But it didn't kill the person. What if he put cowpox germs into people's bodies? Their bodies would learn to recognize the milder germ and fight it. Then the smallpox germ couldn't take hold in their bodies. After all, that's what had happened with the milkmaids.

In 1796 Jenner tried out his idea. He rubbed a milkmaid's cowpox blisters on the arm of a young boy. Later when the boy was exposed to smallpox, he didn't get sick. Edward Jenner had just made the first vaccine for a deadly disease.

1. **What is the main idea?**

   (a) Edward Jenner noticed that milkmaids didn't get smallpox.

   (b) In 1796 a little boy proved that cowpox germs and smallpox germs were related.

   (c) Edward Jenner used cowpox germs to make a vaccine for smallpox.

   (d) Edward Jenner became a doctor.

2. **What is the topic sentence?**

   (a) Edward Jenner had just made the first vaccine for a deadly disease.

   (b) This seemed to prove that cowpox and smallpox germs were similar.

   (c) Later when the boy was exposed to smallpox, he didn't get sick.

   (d) Edward Jenner found that his patients died of smallpox no matter what he did.

3. **What is the best title for this passage?**

   (a) A Deadly Disease

   (b) Edward Jenner and the Milkmaids

   (c) Cowpox and Smallpox

   (d) Using Germs to Stop Smallpox

Passage 2

"We must see her," said the chief's men. "We were ordered to examine every available maiden in the land."

The tribal leader called Singing Brook from her hut. She emerged, holding the wolf skin so tightly about her slender body that only her eyes, hands, and legs were visible. The chief's messengers walked all around her, looking her over and longing to see her face.

"Your hands and legs look normal, and you walk gracefully," the taller of the chief's men said. "So why do you hide beneath that skin?"

Singing Brook did not answer.

"You are deformed! You are hideous," the shorter man cried in an effort to trick her.

But Singing Brook was not fooled. She calmly replied, "No one will see my face until my wedding day. I will only marry a man who loves me for myself and not for my appearance."

"Is your face so disfigured that you cannot bear to show it?" the taller man asked gently.

"I didn't say that. I said that the man I marry must love me no matter what I look like," Singing Brook responded.

1. **What is the main idea?**

   (a) The chief's men are frustrated by Singing Brook when she refuses to show her face.

   (b) Singing Brook is determined to marry a man that isn't concerned with her beauty.

   (c) The chief's men try to trick Singing Brook into showing her face to them.

   (d) Singing Brook is afraid of offending the chief's men.

2. **What is the topic sentence?**

   (a) The chief's messengers walked all around Singing Brook, looking her over and longing to see her face.

   (b) "Is your face so disfigured that you cannot bear to show it?" the taller man asked gently.

   (c) "We were ordered to examine every available maiden in the land."

   (d) "The man I marry must love me no matter what I look like," Singing Brook responded.

3. **What is the best title for this passage?**

   (a) Singing Brook and the Prince

   (b) The Search for the Perfect Bride

   (c) For Love Alone

   (d) The Ugly Bride

Passage 3

Sometimes popular products nearly didn't happen. Post-it Notes® is one example. When Dr. Spencer Silver worked for 3M Company, he made a weak glue. He showed it to another worker named Art Fry. It didn't stick well, and they both agreed it was useless. Silver threw it out. Then, in 1974, Art Fry wished he had a way to temporarily mark the pages in a book. He disliked how ordinary bookmarks fell out. Suddenly, he recalled Silver's weak glue. The two men started to work on bookmarks made with the weak glue. It took them 18 months to get them just right. Then they showed the product to the advertising managers at 3M. They weren't impressed.

Fry looked for other uses for the temporary glue. He wondered how he could use it in his daily life. Fry decided he'd like to put temporary notes on papers in his office. He decided to make notepads. He took his new idea to the advertising department. They didn't think that people would pay more for a sticky notepad. But they decided to give it a try. The company made enough Post-it notepads to sell in four cities. They wanted to see if anyone liked them. Few people bought the notepads. 3M told the stores to give them away just to get people to try them. Almost immediately the stores sold out! Once people tried Post-it Notes®, they really liked them. Today, they are one of 3M's best-selling products.

1. **What is the main idea?**

   ⓐ Post-it Notes®, a popular product, would not have been invented if not for Art Fry's efforts.

   ⓑ Post-it Notes® are the most popular product in 3M history.

   ⓒ Art Fry designed many new products for his employer, 3M.

   ⓓ At first it was hard to get people to buy Post-it Notes®.

2. **What is the topic sentence?**

   ⓐ Fry looked for other uses for the temporary glue.

   ⓑ Sometimes popular products nearly didn't happen.

   ⓒ Once people tried Post-it Notes®, they really liked them.

   ⓓ The company made enough Post-it notepads to sell in four cities.

3. **What is the best title for this passage?**

   ⓐ Giving Products Away Boosts Sales

   ⓑ Successful 3M Products

   ⓒ Making Bookmarks and Notepads

   ⓓ Post-it Notes®: A Sticky Story

Answer Key

Page 5
Passage 1: a   *Passage 2:* c
Page 6
Passage 3: b   *Passage 4:* d
Page 7
Passage 5: a   *Passage 6:* b
Page 8
Passage 7: d   *Passage 8:* c
Page 9
Passage 9: d   *Passage 10:* b
Page 10
Passage 1
Main Idea: a
details: smell bugs underground, can swim for hours, run up to 10 mph, spray oil at enemies, share burrows with other kinds of animals, can live 10 years

Page 11
Passage 2
Main Idea: c
details: Emily fought back tears, worried about explaining, looks at broken vase in horror, vase meant a lot to her mother and grandmother, vase mother's favorite

Passage 3
Main Idea: b
details: grains give energy, meat gives protein, fruits and vegetables provide fiber, minerals, and vitamins A & C, milk/dairy provide calcium and vitamins A & D

Page 12
Passage 4
Main Idea: d
details: if it fell, it had a hard time getting up, five toes for balance, moved slowly due to size, ate leaves from tree tops

Passage 5
Main Idea: a
details: Mom says it's been broken into, table on side, glasses shattered, pots and pans on floor

Page 13
Passage 6
Main Idea: c
details: must stick head inside dead bodies, won't get blood on feathers, lose feathers on head and neck every year

Passage 7
Main Idea: b
details: knights lived inside castle, castles had many means of defense, peasants fled to castle for protection, lords wanted to gain land and become more powerful

Page 14
Passage 8
Main Idea: a
details: Ur too crowded, streets narrow, houses small, rotting food and sewage in streets

Passage 9
Main Idea: c
details: rivers' courses changed, push down Earth's crust, cause U-shaped valleys, drop rocks and soil as it melts

Page 15
Passage 10
Main Idea: d
details: crowded, air not fresh, cramped space, little privacy, dangerous, little chance for escape or rescue

Passage 11
Main Idea: c
details: only footprints are Sue's, thick dust on everything, Sue says no one's been there for a long time

Page 16
Passage 1:
who: Valerie & Mark
did what: went into the vault
when: just before the Earth shook
where: vault's location not given in passage
why: their mother told them to
how: Valerie punched in a code on a keypad

Page 17
Passage 2:
who: Gregor Mendel
did what: discovered genes
when: around 1860
where: at a monastery
why: he wanted to prove parents pass on traits
how: he did experiments on pea plants

Passage 3:
who: Ted & David
did what: found old pallets
when: not given in passage
where: in a field
why: to use in building a tree fort
how: they went looking for things they could use

Page 18
Passage 4:
who: Lakesha and Tamika
did what: Lakesha explained a Kwanzaa principle to Tamika
when: just after Christmas
where: on stairs
why: Tamika asked her
how: by giving an example

Passage 5:
who: Ponce de Leon
did what: looked for Fountain of Youth
when: 1513 and after
where: in Florida, the Bahamas, and Puerto Rico
why: he wanted to be young forever and also to get rich
how: explored new areas

Page 19
Passage 6:
who: scholars
did what: learned how to read Egyptian hieroglyphics
when: 1799-1819
where: not given in passage
why: they wanted to read ancient Egyptian writings
how: used their knowledge of Greek to decode the hieroglyphics on the Rosetta Stone

Passage 7:
who: an elf
did what: found the way to move the boulder
when: not given in passage
where: at entrance to a tunnel
why: he wanted to see inside the tunnel
how: tapping around edges of boulder

Page 20
Passage 8:
who: Garrett Morgan and his brother
did what: rescued trapped workers
when: 1916
where: a tunnel under Cleveland
why: to save their lives
how: used safety hoods (gas masks)

Passage 9:
who: Colby
did what: found an envelope full of money
when: not given in passage
where: on the ground
why: he wanted to see who the envelope belonged to
how: breaking the seal on the envelope

Page 21

Passage 1

b; middle

Passage 2

c; end

Page 22

Passage 3

d; beginning

Passage 4

a; middle

Page 23

Passage 5

c; end

Passage 6

b; beginning

Page 24

Passage 7

a; end

Passage 8

b; middle

Page 25

Passage 9

d; beginning

Passage 10

d; middle

Page 26

Passage 11

b; middle

Passage 12

c; beginning

Page 27

Passage 1: c

Passage 2: d

Page 28

Passage 3: a

Passage 4: a

Page 29

Passage 5: d

Passage 6: b

Page 30

Passage 7: a

Passage 8: b

Page 31

Passage 9: c

Passage 10: d

Page 32

Passage 11: c

Passage 12: b

Page 33

Passage 1: a

Passage 2: d

Page 34

Passage 3: c

Passage 4: c

Page 35

Passage 5: a

Passage 6: b

Page 36

Passage 7: d

Passage 8: c

Page 37

Passage 9: b

Passage 10: a

Page 38

(allow leeway on important words underlined)

Passage 1

words: rose, beautiful, bird, judges

in common: beauty, want, flower

main idea: Every bird wanted the rose, so they asked the judges to choose the most beautiful bird among them.

Passage 2

words: redwood, lumber, qualities, lumber, companies, stop

in common: redwood, lumber, companies, stop

main idea: Lumber companies were cutting down too many redwood trees until Julia Hill stopped them by living in a redwood tree.

Page 39

(allow leeway on important words underlined)

Passage 3

words: Cody, boat, side rail, water ski, instructed, excited, afraid

in common: Cody, boat, water ski, learn, excited, afraid

main idea: At his first water skiing lesson, Cody is excited and a little scared.

Passage 4

words: microwave, oven, faster, food, magnetron, atoms, energy

in common: microwave oven, heat fast, magnetron, energy

main idea: Microwave ovens use magnetrons to heat food fast without wasting energy.

Page 40

Passage 5

A city boy finds it too quiet to sleep in the country until one night a steady noise helps him to fall asleep.

Passage 6

A boy accidentally discovered the first set of Dead Sea Scrolls.

Page 41

Passage 7

Kevin wonders what to do because he doesn't know if his father is injured or has gone to the summit without him.

Passage 8

The number of American bald eagles, the U.S. national bird, is on the rise.

Page 42

The frightened girls on a sailboat hope their craft won't be wrecked on rocks.

Passage 10

People can live through an avalanche if they are found and dug out quickly.

Page 43

Passage 11

Mischief sees gunmen order his friends to hand over their uniforms.

Passage 12

Laundry soaps use chemicals and enzymes to clean clothes.

Page 44

Assessment

Passage 1

   1. c

   2. a

   3. d

Page 45

Assessment

Passage 2

   1. b

   2. d

   3. c

Page 46

Assessment

Passage 3

   1. a

   2. b

   3. d